Relax, God is in Charge

and 77 other inspirational illustrations and thoughts to
enable you to go right, disable you from going wrong,
stick to your ribs, warm the cockles of your heart and
tickle your funny bone.

Created by Meiji Stewart

Illustrated by David Blaisdell

Relax, God is in Charge
© 1995 by Meiji Stewart

ISBN# 0-9647349-0-7

Published in San Diego California by the Keep Coming Back Company
P.O. Box 1204, Del Mar, California 92014
619-452-1386

Illustrated by: David Blaisdell, Tucson, Arizona

Cover and book design: Endore, Ink., San Diego, California

Printed by: Vaughn Printing, Nashville, Tennessee

This book is dedicated to
my daughter, Malia, the puddledancer,
and to her beautiful mother, Julie.

First things first.

If you feel far away from God, guess who moved?

The most important job
in God's world is to be
a loving mom or dad.

God loves me
just the way I am.

Relax, God is in charge.

Fear knocked.
Faith answered.
No one was there.

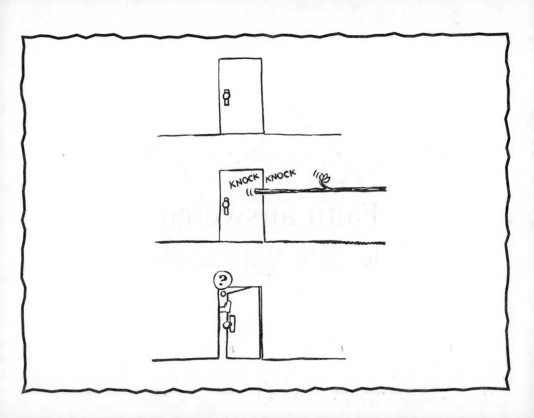

Prayer is the key for
the morning
and the lock for
the night.

I am a precious, fallible
child of God.

Born to be happy,
joyous and free.

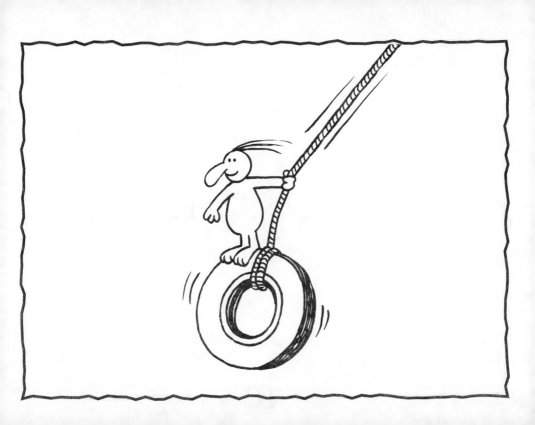

God is never late.

What you are is
God's gift to you.
What you become is
your gift to God.

With God, anything is possible.

Friendship is God's
way of loving us
through someone else.

Smile, God loves you.

Talent on loan from God.

Instead of saying:
"Good God, it's morning."
I say:
"Good morning, God."

God made everyone
different for a reason.

God never closes
a door without
opening another.

I am God's melody of life
and He sings His song
through me.

Nothing is going to
happen today that God
and I can't handle.

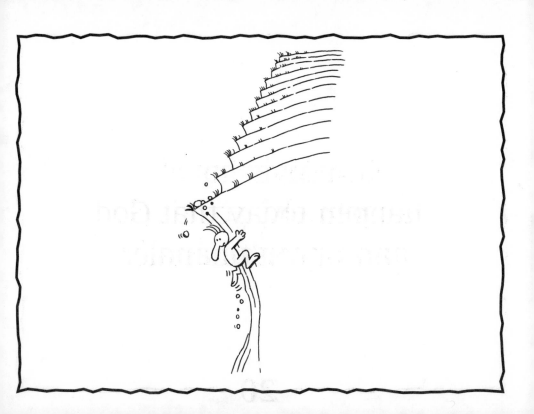

God loves us all,
absolutely, positively
and unconditionally.

God loves me when I work *and* when I play.

God's grace is so bright I gotta wear shades.

I am a masterpiece
created by God.

God is the answer,
whatever the question.

Take time each day to
enjoy God's handiwork.

It's never too late to
make a difference
in a child's life.

We can never really go where God is not, and where He is, all is well.

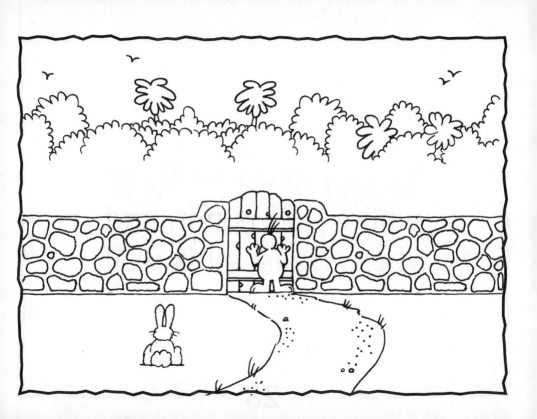

If God is for us, who
can be against us?

No matter what is happening in your life, know that God is waiting for you with open arms.

I can't.
God can.
I think I'll let Him.

If you're too
busy to play,
you're too busy.

Have a good day,
(unless you have
made other plans).

Never walk when
you can dance.

Children are meant to be
seen and heard,
and honored
and cherished
and loved lots and lots
and...

God promises a safe landing,
not a calm passage.

Dare to make your
dreams come true.

A child is God's promise
for the future.

Do your best and then sleep in peace. God is awake.

God created cookies and
milk for a good reason.

A candle loses nothing of its light by lighting others.

God has a purpose and plan for me that no one else can fulfill.

Within every problem
there is an opportunity.

Together we can
do most anything.

God gives us faces.
We create our own
expressions.

The will of God will never take you to where the grace of God will not protect you.

Whoever you are,
whatever you do,
wherever you go,
remember, God loves you.

If you're too busy to pray,
you're too busy.

Children are God's
angels in disguise.

We are responsible for the effort, not the outcome.

We set the sail;
God makes the wind.

Enjoy what you do and you'll never have to work another day.

God will never give
you more than
you can handle.

Know God;
know serenity.
No God;
no serenity.

God grant me the serenity to
accept the things
I cannot change,
the courage to change
the things I can
and the wisdom to
know the difference.

Remember,
God loves you.

With God,
all things are possible.

God and I
are enough.

If you want God to
move a mountain,
you'd better
bring a shovel.

God threw a
party the day
you were born.

Begin to weave
and God will give
you the thread.

Sometimes when God says "no", it's because He has something better in store for you.

There are many
paths to God.

A coincidence is a small miracle in which God chooses to remain anonymous.

The task ahead of
us is never as great as
the power behind us.

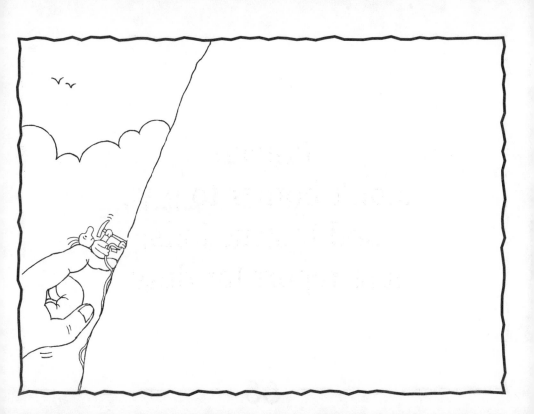

Prayer:
don't bother to give
God instructions;
just report for duty.

Let go and
let God.

I know not what the future holds, but I know who holds the future.

It's my business to do
God's business and it's
His business to take
care of my business.

I have a God of
my very own,
and wherever
I am, He is.

Serenity is not freedom
from the storm, but
peace amid the storm.

God's will is for you to go out and do something for someone else.

God is contagious.
Catch him.

How come you're
always running around
looking for God?
He's not lost.

Call on God,
but row away
from the rocks.

God has only two hands,
so He invented parents.

God put me on earth to accomplish a certain number of things; right now I'm so far behind I will live forever.

We are all
God's children.

Keep Coming Back is a small company in Del Mar, California interested primarily in spiritual, inspirational and 12-step gift products. Many of the illustrations shown in this book are available on one or more of our products. If you want more information, a catalog or have any favorite quotations that you would like to share with us for future books, please contact us at:

Meiji Stewart
Keep Coming Back
P.O. Box 1204
Del Mar, California 92014
Fax 619-452-2797
1-800-522-3383